CELEBRATING THE FAMILY NAME OF GARZA

Celebrating the Family Name of Garza

Walter the Educator

Silent King Books
a WhichHead Entertainment Imprint

Copyright © 2024 by Walter the Educator

All rights reserved. No part of this book may be reproduced in any manner whatsoever without written permission except in the case of brief quotations embodied in critical articles and reviews.

First Printing, 2024

Disclaimer

This book is a literary work; the story is not about specific persons, locations, situations, and/or circumstances unless mentioned in a historical context. Any resemblance to real persons, locations, situations, and/or circumstances is coincidental. This book is for entertainment and informational purposes only. The author and publisher offer this information without warranties expressed or implied. No matter the grounds, neither the author nor the publisher will be accountable for any losses, injuries, or other damages caused by the reader's use of this book. The use of this book acknowledges an understanding and acceptance of this disclaimer.

Celebrating the Family Name of Garza is a memory book that belongs to the Celebrating Family Name Book Series by Walter the Educator. Collect them all and more books at WaltertheEducator.com

USE THE EXTRA SPACE TO DOCUMENT YOUR FAMILY MEMORIES THROUGHOUT THE YEARS

GARZA

Upon the wind, beneath the sun,

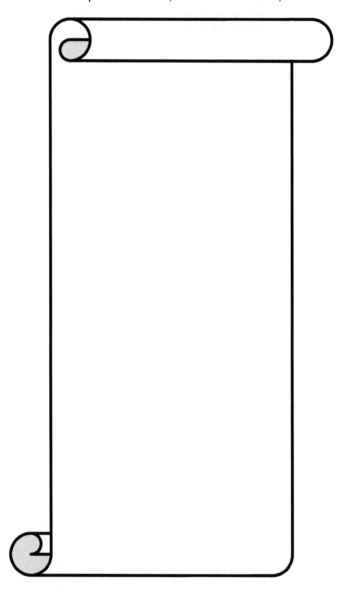

The name of Garza has begun,

A journey vast, from land to sea,

A story rich with destiny.

In skies that burn with golden light,

The Garza soars with wings in flight,

A heron proud, both swift and strong,

With grace that carries it along.

Through marshlands deep and mountains wide,

The Garza name is known with pride,

It moves with quiet, fearless grace,

A noble soul in every place.

From ancient shores of distant lands,

To bustling streets and desert sands,

The Garzas thrived, with heart and will,

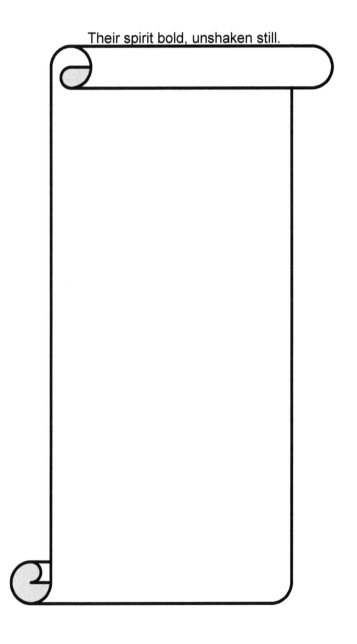
Their spirit bold, unshaken still.

Like birds that glide on currents high,

They found their path beneath the sky,

With eyes that see what others miss,

Their flight a gift, their life a bliss.

Yet not just in the skies they reign,

But in the fields and through the rain,

The Garzas worked with hands of care,

Their legacy was planted there.

With every seed, with every stone,

The name of Garza had been sown,

A harvest rich, a life well-grown,

Their roots deep in the earth unknown.

For Garza means to persevere,

To face the storm and never fear,

To rise from ashes, soar above,

And fill the world with boundless love.

In every heart, the flame remains,

A strength that courses through the veins,

Of those who bear the name with pride,

A family strong, side by side.

They build, they dream, they rise, they stand,

A lineage shaped by heart and hand,

Through every challenge, every test,

They rise again, they do their best.

ABOUT THE CREATOR

Walter the Educator is one of the pseudonyms for Walter Anderson. Formally educated in Chemistry, Business, and Education, he is an educator, an author, a diverse entrepreneur, and he is the son of a disabled war veteran. "Walter the Educator" shares his time between educating and creating. He holds interests and owns several creative projects that entertain, enlighten, enhance, and educate, hoping to inspire and motivate you. Follow, find new works, and stay up to date with Walter the Educator™

at WaltertheEducator.com